This
*My First Communion Journal
In Imitation of St. Therese,
The Little Flower*
belongs to:

_____

Date of First Holy Communion:

_____

Place of First Holy Communion:

_____

_____

© 2011 by Janet P. McKenzie

ISBN 978-1-934185-42-1

Published by
Biblio Resource Publications, Inc.
108½ South Moore Street
Bessemer, MI 49911
www.BiblioResource.com
info@BiblioResource.com

All right reserved. With the exception of short excerpts for critical reviews, no part of this work may be reproduced or transmitted in any form or by any means whatsoever without the written permission of the publisher.

Cover photo © denira - Fotolia.com

Scripture texts in this work are taken from the *New American Bible with Revised New Testament* © 1986, 1970 Confraternity of Christian Doctrine, Washington, D.C. and are used by permission of the copyright owner. All Rights Reserved. No part of the *New American Bible* may be reproduced in any form without permission in writing from the copyright owner.

A **R**ead **A**loud **C**urriculum Enrichment Product
www.RACEforHeaven.com

Printed in the United States of America

General Instructions

(Note: If this journal is being used in conjunction with *Communion with the Saints, A Family Preparation Program for First Communion and Beyond in the Spirit of St. Therese,* be sure to read pages vi through viii in the "General Instructions" of that resource.)

This journal has been constructed in imitation of the "copybooks" used by Celine and Therese Martin as they prepared for their First Holy Communion in 1880 and 1884. These journals were lovingly made by Sr. Agnes of Jesus, the older sister of Celine and Therese Martin, who was at the time a Carmelite nun in the monastery at Lisieux, France. The homemade journals were described in a letter from Sr. Agnes to Therese as copybooks or "little books of preparation" where, under the symbols of flowers, the girls could record their sacrifices and pious thoughts. St. Therese's journal had a cover of blue velvet with her initials embroidered in large white letters. Inside was ". . . one page for each day. Each page was decorated with a border, rays in each of the corners, the date in Gothic illumination, the name of a flower and a short aspiration which the scent of the flower symbolized; it was all done in black and red ink. . . . Prayers to the Child Jesus, the Blessed Virgin, St. Joseph, and the guardian angel preface each of the. . . months."

During her preparation period, Therese was encouraged to turn her heart often to Jesus by reciting the prayers and aspirations in the copybook and to take every opportunity to humble her pride and make sacrifices for the good Jesus. Throughout her sixty-nine day preparation period, she recorded each day the number of times she recited the prayers and, by use of her "sacrifice beads" (a small chaplet of moveable beads—

My First Communion Journal

for which directions are provided at the end of this book), she counted each time she overcame her own desires in order to please Jesus.

Therese, in her letter to Sr. Agnes thanking her for the copybook, tells us the importance she placed in this preparation for Holy Communion: "Every day, I try to perform as many practices as I can, and I do all in my power not to let a single occasion pass by. I am saying at the bottom of my heart the little prayers as often as I can."

At the end of her preparation period, Therese recorded that she had recited the aspirations a total of 2,773 times (an average of about 40 each day) and had performed 1,949 "practices" or little acts of mortification and sacrifice, for an average of 28 each day.

This journal is not an exact replica of the "copybook" used by Therese but it does contain many of the same prayers and aspirations she used, the same idea of flowers inspiring virtue, and the same method of recording prayers recited and sacrifices made. It is up to you to imitate St. Therese in decorating and completing your journal, recording each day the number of times you imitate her heroic efforts by raising your heart to Jesus, and humbling your pride by making small sacrifices at every available opportunity.

I pray that this modern-day "copybook" will bring about the same results that the "little book of preparation" produced in the soul of little Therese so many years ago: the desire to become not a great saint but a little saint by performing each action of daily life with great love and humility and by becoming a little flower in our Lord's bouquet of beloved saints.

Janet P. McKenzie, OCDS
November 1, 2011
Feast of All Saints

Prayers and Aspirations

("For me, *prayer* is an aspiration of the heart, it is a simple glance directed to heaven." – St. Therese)

TO THE CHILD JESUS: (from St. Therese's copybook)
- ✝ "Little Jesus, I love You,"
- ✝ "Little Jesus, don't let me be proud anymore."
- ✝ "Little Jesus, may I always be simple and docile."
- ✝ "My whole heart is Yours, Jesus."
- ✝ "Little Jesus, I kiss You."

TO THE BLESSED VIRGIN:
- ✝ "Holy Mary, help me, like you, to hold Jesus close to my heart."
- ✝ Remember, O most gracious Virgin Mary, that never was it known that anyone who fled to thy protection, implored thy help, or sought thy intercession was left unaided. Inspired by this confidence, I fly unto thee, O Virgin of virgins, my mother; to thee do I come, before thee I stand, sinful and sorrowful. O Mother of the Word Incarnate, despise not my petitions, but in thy mercy hear and answer me. Amen.
- ✝ "O Mary, conceived without sin, pray for us!"

TO ST. JOSEPH:
- ✝ "Dear St. Joseph, teach me to love Jesus as you did."
- ✝ "St. Joseph, foster-father of Jesus, pray for us."

TO MY GUARDIAN ANGEL:
- ✝ "Angel dear, guard and guide me."

St. Therese, the Little Flower

ST. THERESE RECALLS HER FATHER'S SYMBOLIC ACTION AFTER HE GAVE HIS PERMISSION TO ALLOW HER TO ENTER THE CARMELITE MONASTERY:

"Going up to a low wall, he pointed to some *little white flowers*, like lilies in miniature, and plucking one of them, he gave it to me explaining the care with which God brought it into being and preserved it to that very day. While I listened, I believed I was hearing my own story, so great was the resemblance between what Jesus had done for the *little white flower* and *little Therese*. I accepted it as a relic and noticed that, in gathering it, Papa had pulled all its *roots* out without breaking them. It seemed destined to live on in another soil more fertile than the tender moss where it had spent its first days. I placed the little white flower in my copy of the *Imitation [of Christ]* at the chapter entitled: 'One must love Jesus above all things,' and there it is still . . ."

ST. THERESE COMPARES OUR SOULS TO FLOWERS:

"[Jesus] set before me the book of nature; I understood how all the flowers He has created are beautiful, how the splendor of the rose and the whiteness of the lily do not take away the perfume of the little violet or the delightful simplicity of the daisy. I understood that if all flowers wanted to be roses, nature would lose her springtime beauty and the fields would no longer be decked out with little wild flowers.

"And so it is in the world of souls, Jesus' garden. He willed to create great souls comparable to lilies and roses, but He has created smaller ones and these must be content to be daisies or violets destined to give joy to God's glances when He looks down at His feet. Perfection consists in doing His will, in being what He wills us to be.

Read-Aloud Story

The following story—"Shut Up Posy"—is from a book published in 1900, *Story-Tell Lib* by Annie Trumbull Slosson. This book contains little stories told by a orphaned village girl, Elizabeth Rowena Marietta York, "stories out of her own head—kind o' fables that learnt folks things, and helped 'em without being' too preachy."

Once there was a posy. It wasn't a common kind of posy, one that blows out wide open, so everybody can see its outsides and its insides too. But it was one of those posies that grows down the road, back of the sugar shack and doesn't come till way towards fall. They're sort of blue, but real dark, and they look as if they were buds instead of posies—only buds open out and these ones don't. They're all shut up close and tight, and they never, never, never open. Never mind how much sun they get, never mind how much rain or drought, whether it's cold or hot, those posies stay shut up tight, kind of buddy, and not finished and humly. But if you pick 'em open, real careful, with a pin—I've done it—you find they're dreadful pretty inside.

You couldn't see a posy that was finished off better, soft and nice, with pretty little stripes painted on 'em, and all the little things like threads in the middle, such as the open posies have, standing up, with little knots on their tops, oh, so pretty—you never did! Makes you think really hard, that does: leastways makes me. What are they that way for? If they ain't never gonna open out, what the use of havin' the shut-up part so slicked up and nice, with nobody never seein' it? Folks have different names for 'em—dumb foxgloves, blind gentians, and all that, but I always call 'em "the shut-up posies."

Well, it was one of that kind of posy I was goin' to tell you about. It was one of the shut-uppest and the buddiest of all of 'em, all blacky-blue and straight up and down, and shut up fast and tight. Nobody'd ever dream it was pretty inside. And the funniest thing—it didn't know it was so itself! It thought it was a mistake somehow, thought it had ought to have been a posy, and was begun for one, but wasn't finished, and it was terribly unhappy. It knew there were pretty posies all around there, goldenrod and purple daisies and all; and their inside was the right side, and they were proud of it, and held it open, and showed the pretty lining, all soft and nice with the little fuzzy yellow threads standin' up, with little balls on their tip ends. And the shut-up posy felt real bad; not mean and hateful and begrudgin', you know, and wantin' to take away the nice part from the other posies, but sorry, and kind of ashamed.

"Oh, dreary me!" she says—I almost forgot to say it was a girl posy—"dreary me, what a skimpy, humly, awkward thing I am! I ain't more than half made; there ain't no nice, pretty lining inside of me, like those other posies, and only my wrong side shows, and that just plain and common. I can't cheer up folks like the goldenrod and daisies do. Nobody wants to pick me and carry me home. I ain't no good to nobody, and I never shall be."

So she kept on thinkin' these dreadful, sorry thinkin's, and almost wishin' she'd never been made at all. You know it wasn't just at first she thought this way. First she thought she was a bud, like lots of buds all around her, and she counted on opening like they did. But when the days kept passin' by, and all the other buds opened out, and showed how pretty they were, and she didn't open, why, then she got terribly disappointed; and I don't wonder a bit. She'd see the dew

Read-Aloud Story

layin' soft and cool on the other posies' faces, and the sun shinin' warm on 'em as they held 'em up, and sometimes she'd see a butterfly come down and light on 'em real soft, and kind of put his head down to 'em, as if he was kissin' 'em, and she thought it would be powerful nice to hold her face up to all those pleasant things. But she couldn't.

But one day, before she got very old, before she'd dried up or fell of, or anything like that, she saw somebody comin' along her way. It was a man, and he was lookin' at all the posies real hard and particular, but he wasn't pickin' any of 'em. Seems as if he was lookin' for somethin' different from what he saw, and the poor little shut-up posy began to wonder what he was after. By and by she braced up, and she asked him about it in her shut-up, whisperin' voice. And says he, the man, says: "I'm pickin' posies. That what I work at almost all the time. Tain't for myself," he says, "but the one I work for. I'm only his help. I run errands and do chores for him, and it's a particular kind of posy he's sent me for today."

"What for does he want 'em?" says the shut-up posy.

"Why, to set out in his garden," says the man. "He's got the most beautiful garden you ever did see, and I pick posies for it."

"Dreary me," thinks she to herself, "I just wish he'd pick me. But I ain't the kind, I know." And then she says, so soft he can't hardly hear her, "What sort of posies is it you're after this time?"

"Well," says the man, "it's a dreadful singular order I've got today. I got to find a posy that's more handsome on the inside than it is outside, one that folks ain't took no notice of here, 'cause it was kind of humly and odd to look at, not knowin' that inside it was as handsome as any posy on the earth. Seen any of that kind?"

Well, the shut-up posy was dreadful worked up. "Dreary dear!" she says to herself, "now if they'd only finished me off inside! I'm the right kind outside, humly and odd enough, but there's nothin' worth lookin' at inside—I'm certain sure of that." But she didn't say this or anything else out loud, and by and by, when the man had waited, and didn't get any answer, he began to look at the shut-up posy more particular, to see why she was so quiet. And all of a sudden he says, the man did, "Looks to me as if you were somethin' of that kind yourself, ain't you?"

"Oh, no, no, no!" whispers the shut-up posy. "I wish I was, I wish I was. I'm all right outside, humly and awkward, odd as I can be, but I ain't pretty inside—oh! I almost know I ain't."

"I ain't so sure of that myself," says the man, "but I can tell in a jiffy."

"Will you have to pick me to pieces?" says the shut-up posy.

"No, ma'am," says the man. "I've got a way of tellin', the one I work for showed me."

The shut-up posy never knew what he did to her. I don't know myself, but it was somethin' soft and pleasant, that didn't hurt a bit, and then the man he says, "Well, well, well!"

That's all he said, but he took her up real gentle, and began to carry her away.

"Where you takin' me?" says the shut-up posy.

"Where you belong," says the man., "To the garden of the one I work for," he says.

"I didn't know I was nice enough inside," says the shut-up posy, very soft and still.

"They most generally don't," says the man.

MY FIRST COMMUNION JOURNAL IN IMITATION OF ST. THERESE, THE LITTLE FLOWER

Daily Journal Entries

Week 1

> "In two and a half months, Jesus will come down into your heart for the first time! What a lot of work there is to do, what a lot of flowers have to be sown, and how little time there is to do it in!" – Sr. Agnes (Pauline) to her sister Therese upon delivery of her "copybook"

I Pray Today: #_____

Day 1

Virtues for My Garden Today:

_____
_____
_____
_____
_____
_____

My Sacrifices Today: #_____

_____
_____
_____
_____
_____
_____

Week 1

> The SUNFLOWER turns constantly to the sun, following it in its course. In our garden of virtues, first and foremost must be the virtue of FAITH, a light that continually guides us on our way. Tell Jesus today how much you love Him and how much you long to receive Him in Holy Communion.

I Pray Today: #_____

Day 2

Virtues for My Garden Today:

_____
_____
_____
_____
_____
_____

My Sacrifices Today: #_____

_____
_____
_____
_____
_____
_____
_____

Week 1

> *"... Amen, I say to you, if you have faith the size of a mustard seed, you will say to this mountain, 'Move from here to there,' and it will move. Nothing will be impossible for you."* (Matthew 17:20)

I Pray Today: #_____

Day 3

Virtues for My Garden Today:

_____
_____
_____
_____
_____
_____

My Sacrifices Today: #_____

_____
_____
_____
_____
_____
_____
_____

Week 1

> Like the virtue of **HOPE,** the APPLE BLOSSOM brings the promise of the fruit it will bear. Hope must remain alive and active in your heart. You must cultivate it, and nourish it, knowing the fruit it will bear is for all eternity. Tell Jesus today, "Jesus, I trust in You!"

I Pray Today: #_____

Day 4

Virtues for My Garden Today:

My Sacrifices Today: #_____

Week 1

> *"Trust in the Lord with all your heart, on your own intelligence rely not. In all your ways be mindful of him, and he will make straight your paths."* (Proverbs 3:5-6)

I Pray Today: #_____

Day 5

Virtues for My Garden Today:

My Sacrifices Today: #_____

Week 1

> Every flower has a root, a stem, a blossom; the last is the fairest of the three. And it is just the same with the three theological virtues. From the root, which is faith, springs the stem, which is hope; and the lovely flower of LOVE crowns them both. This love is symbolized by the most beautiful flower, the ROSE. You must prove your love of God and your love of neighbor by your actions, by your whole manner of life—in a word, by doing His holy will.

I Pray Today: #_____

Day 6

Virtues for My Garden Today:

_____
_____
_____
_____
_____
_____

My Sacrifices Today: #_____

_____
_____
_____
_____
_____
_____

Week 1

> "I know but one thing now—*to love You*, O Jesus! Glorious deeds are not for me, I cannot preach the Gospel, shed my blood . . . what does it matter? My brothers toil instead of me, and I, *the little child*, I keep quite close to the royal throne, *I love* for those who fight." – St. Therese in *Story of a Soul*

I Pray Today: #_____

Day 7

Virtues for My Garden Today:

My Sacrifices Today: #_____

Week 2

> "On the day of my conversion, love entered into my heart and with it a yearning to forget myself always; from then on, I have been happy."
> – St. Therese in *Story of a Soul*

I Pray Today: #_____

Day 8

Virtues for My Garden Today:

My Sacrifices Today: #_____

Week 2

> "In the Host, the Heart of Jesus is claiming entrance into yours. This gracious Host contains heaven. Is two and a half months too long a time to think of it, and scatter flowers in His pathway?"
> – Sr. Agnes in a letter to Therese

I Pray Today: #_____

Day 9

Virtues for My Garden Today:

_____
_____
_____
_____
_____

My Sacrifices Today: #_____

_____
_____
_____
_____
_____
_____

Week 2

> MARIGOLDS are planted by gardeners to keep pests away from other plants. So too does **PRUDENCE** protect our souls by disposing us to form right judgments about what we must do or not do. Listen to the advice and warnings of others so your decisions are guided and protected by the virtue of prudence.

I Pray Today: #_____

Day 10

Virtues for My Garden Today:

My Sacrifices Today: #_____

Week 2

> *"So now, O children, listen to me; instruction and wisdom do not reject! Happy the man who obeys me, and happy those who keep my ways."*
> (Proverbs 8:32-33)

I Pray Today: #_____

Day 11

Virtues for My Garden Today:

My Sacrifices Today: #_____

Week 2

> The virtue of **JUSTICE** disposes us to give everyone what belongs to him/her. A FLORAL BOUQUET, where many flowers work together, reminds us that everyone has value; we are called to treat everyone equally. In your work and play, you must be fair to everyone and help others to act justly as well.

I Pray Today: #_____

Day 12

Virtues for My Garden Today:

My Sacrifices Today: #_____

Week 2

> *"Do to others what you would have them do to you."*
> (Matthew 7:12)

I Pray Today: # _____

Day 13

Virtues for My Garden Today:

My Sacrifices Today: #_____

Week 2

> Standing tall and strong like flags, GLADIOLAS symbolize the virtue of **FORTITUDE**, which gives us the ability to act courageously, to do what is right under any circumstance. Ask your guardian angel to help you to be strong and steadfast in doing God's will each day in all things and to practice the virtue of fortitude.

I Pray Today: #_____

Day 14

Virtues for My Garden Today:

My Sacrifices Today: #_____

Week 3

> *"Therefore, since we are surrounded by so great a cloud of witnesses, let us rid ourselves of every burden and sin that clings to us and persevere in running the race that lies before us while keeping our eyes fixed on Jesus, the leader and perfecter of faith. . . . "* (Hebrews 12:1-2).

I Pray Today: #_____

Day 15

Virtues for My Garden Today:

My Sacrifices Today: #_____

Week 3

> **TEMPERANCE**—the virtue that helps us to control our desires and to use rightly what is pleasing to us—is characterized by the AZALEA. This flower prefers to grow in temperate climates (regions of moderate temperature) in an area that provides some sun and some shade. Like azaleas, we too grow best when we don't do things to excess and when we do all things for the glory of God rather than to please ourselves. Today, give up something pleasing.

I Pray Today: #_____

Day 16

Virtues for My Garden Today:

My Sacrifices Today: #_____

Week 3

> "On awakening in the morning, I used to think over what would probably occur either pleasing or unpleasant during the day; and if I foresaw only trying events I arose dispirited. Now it is quite the other way; I think of the difficulties and the sufferings that await me, and I rise the more joyous and full of courage the more I foresee opportunities of proving my love for Jesus. . . . Then I kiss my crucifix and say to Him: 'My Jesus, You have worked enough and wept enough during the three-and-thirty years of Your life on this poor earth. Take now Your rest. My turn it is to suffer and to fight.'" – St. Therese in *Counsels and Reminiscences*

I Pray Today:　　　　　　　　　　　#_____

Day 17

Virtues for My Garden Today:

My Sacrifices Today: #_____

Week 3

> "We must practice the little virtues. This is difficult sometimes, but the good God never refuses the first grace, which gives courage to conquer self; if the soul corresponds to it she will find that she immediately receives light. . . . We must first act with courage, then the heart is strengthened and we go from victory to victory." – St. Therese in *Counsels and Reminiscences*

I Pray Today: #_____

Day 18

Virtues for My Garden Today:

My Sacrifices Today: #_____

Week 3

> Fight against the tendency toward pride, planting instead the fragrant violet of **HUMILITY**, causing it to take root, to flourish and blossom. Be like the VIOLET, which blossoms unseen. Grow to resemble this flower. Be free from all pretension and never give yourself haughty airs, nor look with disdain upon others. Submit to advice and correction. Be guided in a childlike spirit by those who are set over you.

I Pray Today: #_____

Day 19

Virtues for My Garden Today:

My Sacrifices Today: #_____

Week 3

> "I beseech thee, my Jesus, to send me some humiliation every time that I attempt to put myself above others." – St. Therese in *Story of a Soul*

I Pray Today: # _____

Day 20

Virtues for My Garden Today:

My Sacrifices Today: #_____

Week 3

> "I am a *very little* soul who can offer only *very little* things to the good God . . . " – St. Therese in *Story of a Soul*

I Pray Today: #_____

Day 21

Virtues for My Garden Today:

My Sacrifices Today: #_____

Week 4

> *"He went down with them and came to Nazareth, and was obedient to them. . ."* (Luke 2:51a) Thus, did Jesus Himself set the example for the virtue of **OBEDIENCE**, that virtue which, like the brilliant CARNATION, should find a place in the garland of virtue that adorns your head, and spreads sweet fragrance all around.

I Pray Today: # _____

Day 22

Virtues for My Garden Today:

My Sacrifices Today: #_____

Week 4

> Obedience means that we subject our will to the will of another. St. Augustine calls obedience "the mother and root of all virtues," and St. Bonaventure calls it "a ship, in which one sails to heaven." You will see that if you learn how to obey early, you will have done a great deal to promote the happiness of your future life.

I Pray Today: #_____

Day 23

Virtues for My Garden Today:

My Sacrifices Today: #_____

Week 4

> "When you cease to consult the sure compass of obedience, the soul loses her way in arid paths where the waters of grace soon fail her."
> – St. Therese in *Story of a Soul*

I Pray Today: #_____

Day 24

Virtues for My Garden Today:

_____
_____
_____
_____
_____
_____

My Sacrifices Today: #_____

_____
_____
_____
_____
_____
_____
_____

Week 4

> "See that you are preparing yourself well for the great day. You must persevere and not stop for an instant, for one moment lost is one flower the less in your garden." – Sr. Agnes in a letter to Therese

I Pray Today: #_____

Day 25

Virtues for My Garden Today:

My Sacrifices Today:				#_____

Week 4

> The DAISY with its plain center, petals, and stem is a symbol of the virtue of **SIMPLICITY**. Like the violet of humility, the daisy is often used by St. Therese to illustrate that we must be content to be little—not to call attention to ourselves but to live God's will quietly, humbly, simply.

I Pray Today: #_____

Day 26

Virtues for My Garden Today:

My Sacrifices Today: #_____

Week 4

> "Just as the sun shines simultaneously on the tall cedars and on each little flower as though it were alone on the earth, so Our Lord is occupied particularly with each soul as though there were no others like it. And just as in nature all the seasons are arranged in such a way as to make the humblest daisy bloom on a set day in the same way, everything works out for the good of each soul." – St. Therese in *Story of a Soul*

I Pray Today: #_____

Day 27

Virtues for My Garden Today:

My Sacrifices Today: #_____

Week 4

> "I understood how all the flowers He had created are beautiful, how the splendor of the rose and the whiteness of the lily do not take away the perfume of the little violet or the delightful simplicity of the daisy. I understood that if all flowers wanted to be roses, nature would lose her springtime beauty, and the fields would no longer be decked out with little wild flowers." – St. Therese in *Story of a Soul*

I Pray Today: #_____

Day 28

Virtues for My Garden Today:

My Sacrifices Today: #_____

Week 5

> "Jesus willed to create great souls comparable to lilies and roses, but He has created smaller ones and these must be content to be daisies or violets destined to give joy to God's glances when he looks down at His feet. Perfection consists in doing His will, in being what he wills us to be." – St. Therese in *Story of a Soul*

I Pray Today: # _____

Day 29

Virtues for My Garden Today:

_____
_____
_____
_____
_____
_____
_____

My Sacrifices Today: #_____

_____
_____
_____
_____
_____
_____
_____

Week 5

> The old-fashioned NARCISSUS possesses an honest fragrance that draws people near. So it is with those who possess **TRUTHFULNESS**, a virtue that includes complete honesty, sincerity, charitable speech, and avoidance of gossip in speech and in hearing. Work to control your tongue, for as St. James notes, *". . . It is a restless evil, full of deadly poison."* (James 3:8b)

I Pray Today: #_____

_____

_____

_____

_____

_____

Day 30

Virtues for My Garden Today:

My Sacrifices Today: #_____

Week 5

> Be on guard against the desire to please at any cost. Strive instead to please God in all your thoughts, words, and actions. Do not allow yourself to be blinded by the success of false men and deceivers. By holding fast to this ideal, you will come to resemble the well-respected and graceful narcissus whose flowers bounce back in the breeze, and you will remain faithful to your friend the truth. It is a wise man who diligently weeds the garden of his own faults, while the fool attends only to the garden of his neighbors.

I Pray Today: # _____

Day 31

Virtues for My Garden Today:

My Sacrifices Today: #_____

Week 5

> "See that you are preparing yourself well for the great day. You must persevere and not stop for an instant, for one moment lost is one flower the less in your garden." – Sr. Agnes in a letter to Therese

I Pray Today: #_____

Day 32

Virtues for My Garden Today:

My Sacrifices Today: #_____

Week 5

> Because it raises us almost to the level of the angels, **CHASTITY** is called "the angelic virtue." Chastity is the LILY, the pearl of virtues. This virtue allows you to avoid all impure and forbidden pleasures. You must regard your body as the temple of the Holy Spirit and desire to keep it pure. It is the lily that is most often associated with St. Joseph, the most pure spouse of Our Lady.

I Pray Today: #_____

Day 33

Virtues for My Garden Today:

My Sacrifices Today: #_____

Week 5

> "I prayed Our Lady of Victories to keep far from me everything that could tarnish my purity for *'to the clean all things are clean.'*" (Titus 1:15)
> – St. Therese in *Story of a Soul*

I Pray Today: #____

Day 34

Virtues for My Garden Today:

My Sacrifices Today: #_____

Week 5

> The tiny flowers of the FORGET-ME-NOT remind us that it is not how big or noticeable our actions need be but how genuine and pious. Cultivate the seeds of the virtue of **PIETY** in your garden. St. Francis de Sales said that one may be considered truly pious who does, out of heartfelt love of God, everything which God commands, which holy Church requires, and which his state in life demands. Piety makes us cheerful and merry. Weave, therefore, the forget-me-not of true piety in the garland of your virtues.

I Pray Today: #_____

_____

_____

_____

_____

_____

Day 35

Virtues for My Garden Today:

My Sacrifices Today: #_____

Week 6

> "Though I do not undervalue beautiful thoughts that seem to unite us to God, I have long understood that we must carefully guard against leaning too much upon them. The most sublime inspirations are nothing without deeds." – St. Therese in *Story of a Soul*

I Pray Today: #_____

Day 36

Virtues for My Garden Today:

My Sacrifices Today: #_____

Week 6

> JASMINE, a fragrant white or yellow flower, corresponds to the virtue of **SWEETNESS**. By the delicate perfume of this virtue, may we encourage all to live a life of devotion to Jesus and to embrace a life of love. "Jesus, teach me love as You loved."

I Pray Today: #_____

Day 37

Virtues for My Garden Today:

My Sacrifices Today: #_____

Week 6

> "A word, a kindly smile, will often suffice to gladden a wounded and sorrowful heart." – St. Therese in *Story of a Soul*

I Pray Today: # _____

Day 38

Virtues for My Garden Today:

My Sacrifices Today: #_____

Week 6

> Its flowers bloom from May to October providing a rich food source for bees and plentiful nitrogen to surrounding plants. As a symbol of the virtue of **GENEROSITY**, CLOVER reminds us that if we let our Triune God protect and sustain us, our lives can make a difference in the lives of those around us. What can you share with others today?

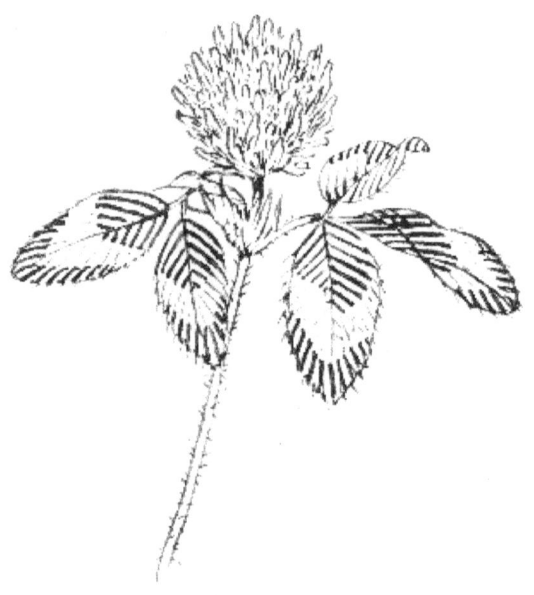

I Pray Today: #_____

Day 39

Virtues for My Garden Today:

My Sacrifices Today: #_____

Week 6

> Scarcely has the winter's snow disappeared from the sunny fields at the approach of spring when the charming, gold-colored DAFFODIL hastens to blossom. This flower is a symbol of **INDUSTRY**, that virtue which speaks to us of exertion, labor, work. Jesus himself worked for thirty years as a carpenter in the workshop in Nazareth. Learn to be faithful to your work and to regard it as honorable.

I Pray Today: # _____

Day 40

Virtues for My Garden Today:

My Sacrifices Today: #_____

Week 6

> *"Go to the ant, O sluggard, study her ways and learn wisdom; For though she has no chief, no commander or ruler, she procures her food in the summer, stores up her provisions in the harvest."*
> (Proverbs 6:6-8)

I Pray Today: # _____

Day 41

Virtues for My Garden Today:

My Sacrifices Today: #____

Week 6

> The virtue of **MORTIFICATION** requires being able to withstand pain and discomfort. It is appropriately represented by the THISTLE plant, a thorny plant with a beautiful flower. Just so is our life with Jesus in that our sacrifices produce something beautiful for God. What are you willing to give up and sacrifice for your friend Jesus today?

I Pray Today: #_____

Day 42

Virtues for My Garden Today:

My Sacrifices Today: #_____

Week 7

> "Far from being like those great souls who from their childhood practice all sorts of penances, I made my mortification consist solely in the breaking of my will, restraining a hasty word, rendering little services to those around me without making anything of it, and a thousand other things of this kind." – St. Therese in *Story of a Soul*

I Pray Today: #____

Day 43

Virtues for My Garden Today:

My Sacrifices Today: #_____

Week 7

> Consider that over 100 million colorful geranium plants are grown and sold throughout the world every year. Each plant, while often different in color and design, still belongs to the GERANIUM family. Now consider that number in souls—100 million souls converted each year! In our **ZEAL FOR SOULS**, we should thirst for many to be converted to the faith and brought to the fullness of truth. Pray for the conversion of a great many souls!

I Pray Today: #_____

Day 44

Virtues for My Garden Today:

My Sacrifices Today: #_____

Week 7

> "*Souls* – dear Lord, we must have souls! Above all, souls of apostles and of martyrs, that through them we may inflame the multitude of poor sinners with love of You." – St. Therese in *Story of a Soul*

I Pray Today: #_____

Day 45

Virtues for My Garden Today:

_____
_____
_____
_____
_____
_____

My Sacrifices Today: #_____

_____
_____
_____
_____
_____
_____

Week 7

> "You must leave nothing undone to make your heart into a heaven where Jesus will want to stay forever! Even now let this beautiful Child be the King, the love of your heart. What is there on this earth lovelier than Jesus? Jesus in His cradle, Jesus sleeping in your heart among the flowers!"
> – Sr. Agnes in a letter to Therese

I Pray Today: #____

Day 46

Virtues for My Garden Today:

My Sacrifices Today: #_____

Week 7

> "The good God does not need years to accomplish His work of love in a soul; one ray from His Heart can, in an instant, make His flower bloom for all eternity." – St. Therese in *Story of a Soul*

I Pray Today: #_____

Day 47

Virtues for My Garden Today:

My Sacrifices Today: #_____

Week 7

> The yellow BUTTERCUP with its five petals and humble appearance is a fitting reminder to us of the five decades of the rosary, which we are to pray each day in honor of the Blessed Virgin Mary. This virtue of **DEVOTION TO MARY** is fitting as she is the most pure mother of our Lord and savior, Jesus. Pray the rosary every day!

I Pray Today: #_____

Day 48

Virtues for My Garden Today:

My Sacrifices Today: #_____

Week 7

> "Sometimes I find myself saying to the Holy Virgin: "Do you know, O cherished Mother, that I think myself more fortunate than you? I have you for Mother and you have not, like me, the Blessed Virgin to love. You are, it is true, the Mother of Jesus, but you have given Him to me, and He, from the cross, gave you to us as our Mother, so we are richer than you." – St. Therese in a letter to her sister Celine

I Pray Today: #_____

Day 49

Virtues for My Garden Today:

My Sacrifices Today: #_____

Week 8

> The beautiful LILAC, with its little buds that group together in fidelity to produce its pleasing spring fragrance, represents the virtue of **FIDELITY IN LITTLE THINGS**. Just so each little action of ours can produce an effect upon others (and upon the entire Church!) that is so pleasing that we are reminded of the great love God has for all of us.

I Pray Today: #_____

Day 50

Virtues for My Garden Today:

My Sacrifices Today: #_____

Week 8

> "I applied myself above all to practice quite hidden little acts of virtue; thus I liked to fold the clothes forgotten by the Sisters, and sought a thousand opportunities of rendering them service."
> – St. Therese in *Story of a Soul*

I Pray Today: #_____

Day 51

Virtues for My Garden Today:

My Sacrifices Today: #_____

Week 8

> The delicate LAVENDER, symbolizing the virtue of **MODESTY**, teaches us that our souls are delicate and we must adorn our bodies—as temples of the Holy Spirit—with clothing that speak of our chastity and purity. In all things, we must act in ways pleasing to our Almighty Creator.

I Pray Today: #____

Day 52

Virtues for My Garden Today:

My Sacrifices Today: #_____

Week 8

> A Sister said that in heaven Therese would be a beautiful flower, resplendent with light. "Oh no," Therese replied, "you know how in pretty bouquets they conceal some moss to make the flowers stand out; well, I shall be a little bit of moss to set off the beauty of the elect." - *Counsels and Reminiscences*

I Pray Today: # _____

Day 53

Virtues for My Garden Today:

My Sacrifices Today: #_____

Week 8

> The virtue of **ATTACHMENT TO GOD** is aptly portrayed by the clinging vines of the MORNING GLORY whose flowers open each morning, turning toward the rising sun. Begin each day by renewing your attachment to God in prayer. Cling to Him throughout the day and close each day with joyful praise of the One who loves you.

I Pray Today: #_____

Day 54

Virtues for My Garden Today:

My Sacrifices Today: #_____

Week 8

> "In this world we must not become attached to anything—not even things the most innocent, for they fail us at the moment when we are least expecting it. The eternal alone can satisfy us." – St. Therese in a letter to Sr. Marie

I Pray Today: #_____

Day 55

Virtues for My Garden Today:

My Sacrifices Today: #_____

Week 8

> BLUEBELL flowers remind us of the church bells that call us to prayer and to Mass. We must constantly be turning our thoughts and attention to God and to prayer, to increase our **DESIRE FOR HEAVEN**. The bluebells softly chime in the gentle breeze reminding us of God's call to focus on our end goal—heaven. Think of God and the treasures of heaven often.

I Pray Today: #____

Day 56

Virtues for My Garden Today:

My Sacrifices Today: #_____

Week 9

> "The certainty of going away one day far from the sad and dark country had been given me from the day of my childhood. I did not believe this only because I heard it from persons more knowledgeable than I, but I felt in the bottom of my heart real longings for this most beautiful country." – St. Therese in *Story of a Soul*

I Pray Today: #_____

Day 57

Virtues for My Garden Today:

My Sacrifices Today: #_____

Week 9

> "Do not grow tired of gardening. The days pass quickly and Jesus is drawing near." Sr. Agnes in a letter to Therese

I Pray Today: #____

Day 58

Virtues for My Garden Today:

My Sacrifices Today: #_____

Week 9

> The virtue of **GRATITUDE** prompts us to be thankful for our blessings and the love of Jesus. The LILY OF THE VALLEY with its sweet-smelling, bell-shaped flowers reminds us that Jesus cares for all creation. In addition, it was these little flowers that inspired St. Therese to call herself, "The Little White Flower." How can you express your gratitude to Jesus for His love and to St. Therese for her "Little Way"?

I Pray Today: #_____

Day 59

Virtues for My Garden Today:

My Sacrifices Today: #_____

Week 9

> "Going up to a low wall, my father pointed to some *little white flowers*, like lilies in miniature, and plucking one of them, he gave it to me explaining the care with which God brought it into being and preserved it to that very day. While I listened I believed I was hearing my own story, so great was the resemblance between what Jesus had done for the *little flower* and *little Therese*." – St. Therese in *Story of a Soul*

I Pray Today: #____

Day 60

Virtues for My Garden Today:

My Sacrifices Today: #_____

Week 9

> Walking one day in the garden with one of her sisters, Therese paused to enjoy the fascinating sight of a little white hen sheltering its chickens beneath its wings. . . . Looking at her sister with a heavenly expression, she said: "What a touching comparison the Lord chose in order to make us believe in His tenderness. That is just what He has done for me all my life: *He has wholly hidden me beneath His Wings!* . . . Ah! The good God does well to veil Himself from my sight, to show me the effects of His Mercy rarely, as such consolations would, I feel, be more than I could bear." – St. Therese in *Story of a Soul*

I Pray Today: #_____

Day 61

Virtues for My Garden Today:

My Sacrifices Today: #_____

Week 9

> The colorful PANSY, with its ability to bloom in the spring, summer, and fall seems to radiate the virtue of JOY. It is easy as a Christian to be joyful: Put **J**esus first, then **o**thers, then **y**ourself.

I Pray Today: # _____

Day 62

Virtues for My Garden Today:

My Sacrifices Today: #_____

Week 9

> "I hope you are continuing to adorn your little heart for the *sweet visit* you're preparing for. My darling, don't let a single flower escape. It would be bad to see in your garden a little corner of soil not in bloom. Time is passing; be courageous! Oh! If you could see the beautiful reward awaiting you! If you only knew, dear baby, what joy it is to have Jesus in one's heart for the first time!" – Sr. Agnes in a letter to Therese

I Pray Today: #____

Day 63

Virtues for My Garden Today:

_____
_____
_____
_____
_____
_____

My Sacrifices Today: #_____

_____
_____
_____
_____
_____
_____
_____

Week 10

> "It is a great joy to me, not only when others find me imperfect, but above all when I feel that I am so; compliments, on the contrary, cause me nothing but displeasure." – St. Therese in *Story of a Soul*

I Pray Today: # ____

Day 64

Virtues for My Garden Today:

My Sacrifices Today: #_____

Week 10

> "It seems to me that if a little flower could speak, it would tell simply what God has done for it without trying to hide its blessings. It would not say, under the pretext of a false humility, it is not beautiful or without perfume, that the sun has taken away its splendor and the storm has broken its stem when it knows that all this is untrue. . . . She knows that nothing in herself was capable of attracting the divine glances, and His mercy alone brought about everything that is good in her." – St. Therese in *Story of a Soul*

I Pray Today: #_____

Day 65

Virtues for My Garden Today:

My Sacrifices Today: #_____

Week 10

> On your First Communion Day, the Child Jesus "will smile at you, His little hands will be full of roses for you, and the angels will pull off their thorns. There will be nothing to hurt you, everything will be sunny and smiling for you, and the morning will be like a morning in heaven." – Sr. Agnes in a letter to Therese

I Pray Today: #_____

Day 66

Virtues for My Garden Today:

My Sacrifices Today: #_____

Week 10

> "When we commit a fault we must not think it due to a physical cause, such as illness or the weather, we must attribute this fall to our imperfection, but without ever growing discouraged."
> – St. Therese in *Story of a Soul*

I Pray Today: # _____

Day 67

Virtues for My Garden Today:

My Sacrifices Today: #_____

Week 10

> "If there are lots of flowers in your garden, if everything is ready for the great day, you may be sure that Jesus will not come empty handed either! If you only knew what treasures are hidden in the tiny Host for a well-prepared First Communion!"
> – Sr. Agnes in a letter to Therese

I Pray Today: # _____

Day 68

Virtues for My Garden Today:

My Sacrifices Today: #_____

Week 10

> In a few hours the great day will be here . . . and then Jesus will come and live in your blossoming garden. . . . I imagine Jesus saying: 'I am your Jesus, and I have just left heaven to visit the little flower garden that you have been getting ready for me these last three months. I'm longing to walk there and rest in it. Your little heart will be my heaven, and I shall like it better than the throne of gold and jewels that belongs to me in heaven. Now I shall never again leave the cradle of lilies where I am going to sleep; I shall remain there forever . . . unless sin should force me to leave it.'" – Sr. Agnes in a letter to Therese

I Pray Today: #_____

Day 69

Virtues for My Garden Today:

My Sacrifices Today: #_____

WHAT I WANT TO REMEMBER ABOUT MY FIRST HOLY COMMUNION

"In Commemoration of This Most Holy Sacrament"

Bibliography

Clarke, John, O.C.D., Translator. *St. Thérese of Lisieux General Correspondence, Volume 1, 1877-1890*. Washington, D.C.: Washington Province of Discalced Carmelites, Inc., 1982.

Descouvemont, Pierre and Halmuth Nils Loose. *Therese and Lisieux*. Grand Rapids, Michigan: Wm. B. Eerdmans Publishing Company, 1996.

Lasance, Rev. Francis X. *Our Lady Book*. New York, New York: Benziger Brothers, 1924.

Lasance, Rev. Francis X. *The Little Girl's Guide, Counsels and Devotions for Girls in the Ordinary Walks of Life*. New York, New York: Benziger Brothers, 1905.

Mother Agnes of Jesus, O.C.D. *Little Counsels of Mother Agnes of Jesus, OCD*. Parnell, Michigan: Ideal Pub-lishing Company, 1982.

Piat, Fr. Stéphane-Joseph, O.F.M. *The Story of a Family, The Home of St. Thérèse of Lisieux*. Rockford, Illinois: Tan Books and Publishers, 1994.

Slosson, Annie Trumbull. Story-Tell Lib. New York, New York: Charles Scribner's Sons, 1900.

St. Thérese of Lisieux. *Story of a Soul, The Autobiography of St. Thérese of Lisieux*. Washington, D.C.: Institute of Carmelite Studies, 1976.

The Little Flower of Jesus, Carmelite of the Monastery of Lisieux, 1873-1897. *Thoughts of the Servant of God, Therese of the Child Jesus*. New York, New York: P. J. Kenedy & Sons, 1915.

My First Communion Journal

How to Make Sacrifice Beads

Materials:
- 10 pony beads
- 1 cross, approximately 1¼"
- 1 religious medal, approximately 1"
- 22" piece of waxed string

1. You will need to attach your medal to the center of the string. Fold the string in half and pass the fold through the ring on the medal; then pass the two loose ends of the string through the loop. Now your medal is secured to the center of the string.
2. Take your first pony bead and thread it onto the string by passing one end of the string through the hole in the pony bead and the other end of the string through the hole from the opposite side of the bead.
3. The string that came out the left side of bead #1 should pass back through the hole in bead #2 from left to right and the string that exited bead #1 on the right should be passed through bead #2 from right to left.
4. Repeat step #3 for the eight remaining beads.
5. Once all ten beads are on the string, knot the two loose ends of the string together.
6. Finally, attach the cross in the same way the medal was attached to the other end. To do this, pass the knot-ted end through the loop ring (hole) in the cross then pass the opposite end of the string (the end with the medal and beads on it) through this loop and pull taut.

To use: Start with all the beads at one end. Each time you make any sacrifice, slide one bead down to the opposite end. By keeping the beads with you all the time, it will serve as a reminder to make sacrifices as St. Therese did to honor Jesus' great sacrifice for us.

(Used with permission from http://www.craftelf.com)

Other RACE for Heaven Sacramental Prep Resources

Communion with the Saints: A Family Preparation Program for First Communion and Beyond in the Spirit of St. Therese imitates St. Therese of the Child Jesus and her family who studied and prayed for sixty-nine days in anticipation of Therese's First Holy Communion. Modeling this preparation, the *Communion with the Saints* program will help any family find renewed fervor in the reception of the Eucharist. This resource includes a chapter-by-chapter study of the following four books:

- *The Little Flower, The Story of Saint Therese of the Child Jesus*—to provide the foundation of God's love for us and to encourage a desire for holiness

- *The Children of Fatima and Our Lady's Message to the World*—to show the sinfulness of our world and the need to avoid sin

- *The Patron Saint of First Communicants, The Story of Blessed Imelda Lambertini*—to inspire devotion to the Sacrament of Holy Communion

- *The King of the Golden City* by Mother Mary Loyola — to illustrate Jesus' Presence as a source of grace necessary to live a holy life

Each of the sixty-nine days of preparation includes read-aloud selections with enrichment activities, meditational readings, catechism lessons, and plenty of practical application to promote a growth in holiness and sanctity. Week-end suggestions include a list of over thirty-five family projects. The use of *My First Communion Journal* is encouraged with this program.

The King of the Golden City Study Edition is a new edition of a book that was originally published in 1921. This

My First Communion Journal

treasure of a book was written in response to a student's appeal for instructions along with "little stories" to help her prepare for Holy Communion. To fulfill this request, Mother Loyola of the Bar Convent in York, England, wrote a simple story that illustrates Jesus' desire to share an intimate relationship with each one of His children. This new edition contains some updated language but, quite deliberately, does not contain any pictures. Readers, as they progress through this story, will form a mental image of their King, one as unique and personal as their own relationship with Him. The study sections assist with the allegory, connect to the Bible as well as to the catechism, and explore the art of prayer in the spirit of the three Carmelite Doctors of the Church. Although written over ninety years ago for a young child, this book remains a timeless masterpiece of Catholic literature suitable for all ages. (Also available as a study guide only)

The Good Shepherd and His Little Lambs Study Edition is a simply told Catholic tale of four children who meet with their beloved aunt for "First Communion talks." More than a story, it is a First Communion primer that takes the tenets of the catechism and, through naturally-flowing conversations, relates them in the language of little ones to authentic Christian living. As Mrs. Bosch explains, "We might learn the catechism all the way through beautifully, and at the end find ourselves still very stiff and clumsy about loving our Lord. When He comes to us, we don't want to welcome Him into our souls only with answers out of the catechism, do we?" Enriched by appropriate Biblical passages, points of doctrine, and prayers, this story-primer is an enjoyable and effective read-aloud that will prepare the Good Shepherd's little lambs to worthily receive Him in the Holy Eucharist.

A Reconciliation Reader-Retreat: Read-Aloud Lessons, Stories, and Poems for Young Catholics Preparing for Confession provides a basic doctrinal explanation and review of the Sacrament of Reconciliation as well as

Other RACE for Heaven Resources

a Gospel examination of conscience—a seven-day read-aloud formation retreat. To help the lessons come alive and to enable young Catholics to more readily apply these doctrines to their own daily lives, the lessons have been supplemented with pertinent short stories and poems. Each lesson contains reflection questions, a family prayer, and a "Gospel Examination of Conscience" that is formulated according to the dictates of the *Catechism of the Catholic Church*. This reader-retreat will not only enrich and deepen the sacramental experience for each member of your family but it will also provide several tools to help you recommit to leading a virtuous life and to grow together in holiness.

The Outlaws of Ravenhurst Study Edition contains a classic story of the persecution of Scottish Catholics that was first written in 1923 and was revised and reprinted in 1950. This 2009 edition of Sr. M. Imelda Wallace's *Outlaws of Ravenhurst* contains the revised story of 1950 plus chapter-by-chapter aids to assist readers in assimilating the book's strong Catholic elements into their own lives. The study section focuses on critical thinking, integration of biblical teachings, and the study of the virtuous life to which Christ calls us as mature Catholics. With its emphasis on virtues (theological and moral plus the gifts and fruits of the Holy Spirit), the spiritual and corporal works of mercy, and the Beatitudes, *Outlaws of Ravenhurst Study Edition* is a fun and effective catechetical tool for Catholics preparing for the Sacrament of Confirmation. (Also available as a study guide only)

The Family that Overtook Christ Study Edition: The Story of the Family of St. Bernard of Clairvaux is an excellent read for young adults who are preparing to receive the Sacrament of Confirmation. In this exciting chronicle of the life of twelfth-century knights, we have an entire family of nine saints who lay before us their individual means of achieving intimate union with Christ. Learn with the Fontaines family how to supernaturalize the natural, develop a

God-consciousness, and attain sanctity by being yourself. Perfect for high-school read-aloud (or adult study), this new study edition has over 250 footnotes for increased comprehension and provides discussion/meditation points to promote the art of spiritual conversation. The appendix lists formulas of Catholic doctrine that are essential for confirmands not only to know but also to incorporate into their own spiritual lives.

A Confirmation Reader-Retreat: Read-Aloud Lessons, Stories and Poems for Young Catholics utilizes chapters from two excellent out-of-print Catholic books for children (*I Belong to God, Great Truths in Simple Stories for Children and Lovers of Children* by Lillian Clark; and *Children's Retreats in Preparation for First Confession, First Holy Communion, and Confirmation* by Rev. P.A. Halpin). This book provides a basic doctrinal review of the Sacrament of Confirmation as well as prayer experiences—a nine-day read-aloud retreat/novena. The reprinted material has been supplemented with short stories and poems that provide insights in applying catechetical doctrines to the daily life of young Catholics. Each lesson concludes with "I Talk with God"—a section that encourages readers (of all ages) to deepen their relationship with each of the Three Persons of the Blessed Trinity. Reflection questions promote the habit of spiritual conversation within your family—to encourage family members to discuss holy topics—and to help you grow together in holiness. Additionally, a traditional novena to the Holy Spirit is included.

To Order: Email info@RACEforHeaven.com or place an order from RACEforHeaven.com. Discover, MasterCard, VISA, PayPal, American Express, checks, and money orders are accepted.

www.ingramcontent.com/pod-product-compliance
Lightning Source LLC
LaVergne TN
LVHW011421080426
835512LV00005B/194